Chicago Werner Company

Aids to Self-Culture in the Americanized Encyclopedia Britannica for the Home Educational Circle

-

Chicago Werner Company

Aids to Self-Culture in the Americanized Encyclopedia Britannica for the Home Educational Circle

ISBN/EAN: 9783337226084

Printed in Europe, USA, Canada, Australia, Japan

Cover: Foto ©Lupo / pixelio.de

More available books at **www.hansebooks.com**

GUIDE

TO

SELF-CULTURE

IN THE

Americanized Encyclopedia Britannica.

Aids to Self-Culture

IN THE

AMERICANIZED
ENCYCLOPEDIA BRITANNICA

FOR THE

HOME EDUCATIONAL CIRCLE

"Attempt the end, and never stand to doubt;
Nothing's so hard but search will find it out."
—HERRICK.

THE STAR SAYINGS

ST. LOUIS, MO.

1895

Self-Culture and Success

IN THE

HOME EDUCATIONAL CIRCLE.

What is the touchstone of success? Where is the key that will unlock the treasures of fortune, the star that will guide the wanderer along the rugged pathway to the happiness of hopes achieved? There have been many answers to these questions since in the middle ages the alchemists bent for years over the crucible in the vain hope of finding some elixir that would transmute base metals into gold, or since Ponce de Leon lost his life in the new world in his foolish quest for the fabled spring whose waters would restore to his age the strength and elasticity of vanished youth.

In these modern days men go on fools' errands after fortune, wasting the hours they might devote to work and study in chasing some

WILL-O'-THE-WISP,

some vagrant phantom which they hope will for them transmute the base metals of failure and wasted opportunities into the gold of success; but the men who succeed and the men who fail alike will say that Knowledge is Power, and that with no other weapon can the young soldier fight the battle of life. Each man who reads these lines must admit the truth of this assertion. It is the lesson of the times and of all time. But, some will say to themselves, "the pathway to knowledge is too hard; let others plod along in that dull, stupid way,

3

I will trust to luck to meet some opportunity that will bring me more fortune and success than all their toilings." Never was greater mistake. The man who never does anything but wait for opportunities will not recognize them when he sees them. It is

WORK AND STUDY

that sharpen the wits and strengthen the muscles of body and mind to meet the opportunity when it comes. Luck is seldom a great factor in life. The towering genius who can disregard ordinary rules and carve out his own fortunes by mere force of personality is only one of hundreds of thousands; he may appear but once in a century.

The man who stops a runaway horse in the street, gaining credit and, perhaps, advancement, has to have something more than the opportunity. He has to have the quickness of eye and hand, the courage and strength that come only with training. The falling of an apple at his feet revealed to Sir Isaac Newton in a flash the great principle of gravitation, which revolutionized science; but he had been preparing himself unconsciously for that moment by years of study of the laws of matter. Apples had fallen at the feet of other men before Newton, but they spoke no such ringing lesson, because the other men had not the training to hear it. Sir Samuel Brown conceived the idea of the suspension bridge from seeing a spider's web swinging in the breeze, but he had been a student of engineering and was then devoting himself to the study of bridge building. He was READY!

Some may admit the value of knowledge, of scientific training in any pursuit of life, but despair of attaining it because of lack of means, lack of time, absence of early educational advantages and fancied lack of ability. To all such and to all others who have the

AMBITION FOR MENTAL IMPROVEMENT

and for betterment in life which every well regulated
man should have, we wish to point out a Royal Road to
Knowledge. We shall show them the pathway and all
they will need to contribute to the task will be the
attributes of industry and perseverance. "Industry and
perseverance." Few words are more pregnant with
meaning. Little real success was ever won in this
world without them. Stephenson worked for 15 years
in making the first successful locomotive. It took
Watt 30 years to perfect his invention of the con-
denser for steam engines. Buffon, the famous naturalist,
rewrote his "Epochs of Nature" eleven times before he
was satisfied to send it to the printer. These are but a
few of the thousands of instances that might be cited
to show that great works, great ideas and great inven-
tions were the result of long-continued labor. It should
not be forgotten either that the labor was that of men
who had a definite aim in view, and devoted all their
energies to following out that particular line of effort.
Watt could never have invented his steam engine if he
had not had a very clear idea of what he wanted to do
and stuck to it manfully to the end. It is certain, then,
that something else is needed besides industry and perseverance to reach the longed-for goal of success, and
that is, a *definite purpose.* Part of the advantage of
the

ROYAL ROAD TO LEARNING

that we here point out is the aid it will give those
who have no fixed aim in life in selecting one that is
suited to their taste and energies. It cannot be disputed
that men work best and achieve the best results if
they take an active interest in the professional, commercial or industrial task in which they are engaged.

If they look upon their work as a drudgery, to be laid aside with a feeling of relief at the earliest possible moment, they will rarely be able to accomplish any lasting good to themselves or to humanity.

It is of the first importance to the young man starting out in life to select an occupation that will be congenial and inspire his best energies. But, knowing nothing of the world, he too frequently leaves this selection to others, or to chance, only to find out later that he has made a mistake. Many men who find that they have made this mistake, in selecting a career, weakly succumb to circumstances and make no effort to surmount them. But it is never too late to learn, and a perusal of the following pages will show that this royal road to learning is valuable, not only in guiding the first footsteps of the beginner aright, but in enabling the older traveler in the caravan of life who has taken the wrong road to reach the right one where his tastes and energies will have free play, and he may develop the best that is in him for himself and for others.

YOU TEACH YOURSELF.

But do not imagine that because this is the royal road to learning it is a smooth descending highway; that you may follow it as easily as one may float down a river. It is a royal road because it teaches you to teach yourself, and of all culture, self-culture is the highest and most valuable. What you master yourself remains with you longest, because it becomes part of yourself, a weapon fitted to your hand and brain for the struggle of life. "The best culture," said a scholar of ripe experience, "is not obtained from teachers when at school or college so much as by our own diligent self-education when we have become men."

Valuable as that school and college training is, it is not necessary in the scheme of life of one who will follow the path to the royal road to knowledge to be laid down in these pages. Some of the most successful leaders in every profession and every industry have been what are called "self-made men," because they had no advantages of early training and no one to give them a start in life. Henry Wilson, who became vice-president of the United States, was a poor boy whose parents apprenticed him to a farmer when he was ten years old. And yet, in spite of the hard work of the farm Henry Wilson found time before he was twenty-one to read a thousand books and lay the foundation of the ripe learning that gave him power and prominence in public affairs.

BETTER CHANCE THAN LINCOLN'S.

The great beauty and advantage of this royal road to learning is that the journey may be prosecuted along with the daily task of life, whatever it may be. The man or boy engaged in daily occupation for the support of himself or of others will find through an earnest effort to seize the opportunities pointed out in these pages, far better advantages than Henry Wilson had on the farm, or than Abraham Lincoln had, studying in his cabin by the light of a pine knot after a hard day's work at the most irksome tasks. We cannot all be Abraham Lincolns or Henry Wilsons; a Watt, a Stephenson or an Edison; but we can all make the most of ourselves and the talent that has been given us. The man or youth who does not study to improve his mind, to increase his stock of information, is like a man who, with a large sum of money, does nothing with it, does not go into business or put it out at interest, but keeps it in his private coffers. His fund will gradually disappear and he will find himself, in time, as poor as his neighbor without anything. In the same way the man who does not improve his mind by study, strengthen his skill and knowledge of his trade or profession by constant research, will find himself poor in the end, far outstripped in the race of life by the man who started with no more natural intelligence but who seized and improved every opportunity to add to his store of learning and enrich his mental capacity.

AN HOUR OR TWO A DAY

at the work bench, at the desk, or at the fireside at home, devoted to study, will repay interest a hundred fold on the investment. "Take care of the cents and the dollars will take care of themselves," is an old saying. Let the economist of time take care of the minutes and he will find that the hours are not wasted. Do not shrink from any fancied difficulties, but realize how incomparably easier is the task of acquiring knowledge on any special or on general subjects in these days of good books and cheap books, than when Lincoln and Wilson surmounted the greater difficulties that confronted them.

The student who decides to enroll himself in The Home Educational Circle, need not fear that after years of study he must shun comparison with the graduates of schools and universities, with those whose means and leisure may have enabled them to employ expensive tutors. He who possesses a copy of that great work, "The Americanized Encyclopedia Britannica" and utilizes the following hints to its intelligent study, need fear no comparison with the product of expensive university training. He will have levied tribute on the brightest minds of the age and of all ages. The concentrated

LEARNING OF THE CENTURIES

will be placed at his disposal—the ripest thoughts of all philosophers, the tenets of all theologies, the principles of every science, the rules of every profession and the practical details of every industry. The world will be his curriculum and its brightest and best thinkers will be his instructors. The rise and fall of nations, the triumphs of state-craft and diplomacy, the influence on action and thought of great discoveries in science, will all be laid bare to his delighted view. The growth of the arts, the latest improvements in handicrafts, the principles of law, of medicine, of commerce and of agriculture will be unfolded in their due and proper order before him. The wealth of the world will be his, from which to pluck the jewels he admires the most to set in his own crown of knowledge.

Let not the wide extent of the field, wide as life itself, deter the beginner. It is for him to pick and choose. He can set himself the ambitious but glorious task of acquiring something of universal knowledge, or he can select a field of research in which he will find most pleasure and profit. The great advantage of this field of study is the prodigality and thoroughness of its resources. The student of law or medicine, the embryo architect, artist, botanist, farmer, mechanic or merchant, can not only find here the principles that will fit him for the prosecution of his chosen line of endeavor but can acquire

THE BROAD CULTURE

given by general knowledge that will sharpen his faculties and increase his strength in his special field.

The Americanized Encyclopedia Britannica is an inexhaustible mine of wealth to the earnest student from which he may delve at will for the bright nuggets of the gold of wisdom. It is an endless orchard in which he may wander, plucking from every variety of the tree of knowledge the ripe fruit nourished by the work and thought of all the sages of the universe.

Assuming that the student has not determined for himself the vocation he desires to follow in life; or that having reached mature years his vocation is fixed to his satisfaction and that he desires to gain knowledge for his own sake rather than any especial use to which he might put it, it will be instructive to append a brief list of some of the subjects he will find discussed in the great works, all of them thoroughly, some of them exhaustively, and all by specialists who are masters of the particular subject of which each of them treats. The list does not begin to exhaust the wealth of Britannica, it is no more than a bouquet of flowers picked from an extensive garden. But the selection will speak for itself. Here it is:

GENERAL HOME STUDIES.

Aëronautics,	Artesian Wells,	Census,
Æsthetics,	Assaying,	China,
Agriculture,	Astronomy,	Chronology,
Alchemy,	Balance of Power,	Charter,
Ambassador,	Ballot,	Charta, Magna,
Ambulance,	Banking,	Condottieri,
American Literature,	Battle,	Corea,
Ammunition,	Baths,	Communism,
Anatomy,	Bibliography,	Confederate States,
Animals,	Bimetallism,	Cremation,
Anthropology,	Biology,	Cryptography,
Aquarium,	Birds,	Darwinian Theory,
Archæology,	Bookkeeping,	Dietetics,
Architecture,	Botany,	Diplomacy,
Argonauts,	Building,	Distillation,
Arithmetic,	Cannibalism,	Drama,
Army,	Carbonari,	Drawing,
Arsenal,	Carthage,	Dream,
Art,	Catacombs,	Dynamics,

Earth,
Education,
Elections,
Electricity,
England, Language
and Literature,
Ethics,
Evolution,
Exchange,
Extradition,
Finance,
Fine Arts,
Forestry,
Free Masonry,
Free Trade,
Genealogy,
Geodesy,
Geography,
Geology,
Grammar,
Greenback Party,
Herbarium,
Histology,
History,
Horticulture,
Industrial Exhibitions
Know Nothings,
Logic,
Magnetism,
Mechanics,
Mensuration,

Metallurgy,
Metaphysics,
Meteorology,
Microscopy,
Mineralogy,
Monroe Doctrine,
Mound Builders,
Municipality,
Mythology,
National Debt,
Navigation,
Numismatics,
Optics,
Ornithology,
Painting,
Philology,
Philosophy,
Phonetics,
Photography,
Phrenology,
Physical Science,
Physiology,
Pneumatics,
Polar Regions,
Political Conventions,
Political Economy,
Population,
Prison Systems,
Prohibition Party,
Public Health,
Public Lands,

Pyrotechny,
Railways,
Registration,
Republican Party,
Sanitary Science,
Shorthand,
Signal Service,
Slavery,
Sleep,
Sociology,
State's Rights,
Statistics,
Tariff,
Taxidermy,
Telegraphy,
Telephone,
Telescope,
Theology,
Tournaments,
Treason,
Treaties,
Ultimatum,
Vandals,
Vegetable Kingdom,
Veterinary Science,
Veto,
Viticulture,
Whig and Tory,
Whig Party,
Zoölogy.

The reader will soon discover that the subjects given in the above list are general titles, covering extended fields of inquiry. Many of the articles like those on "banking," "sculpture," "political economy," "anatomy," "mechanics," "electricity," etc., are followed through all their ramifications with full treatises on co-ordinate or subordinate themes. The student can select from the best topics which appeal to his fancy or are germane to his daily duties, feeling assured that even a cursory reading, diligently followed up, will widen his information, quicken his intelligence and, best of all, increase his thirst for knowledge, for the appetite for learning grows on what it feeds. A continued course of reading will strengthen the student, be he young or old, for the battle of life which is yearly growing more difficult because of the increase of competition in every field of endeavor. He will realize to the full the truth of the saying that "learning is wealth to the poor, an honor to the rich, an aid to the young and a support and comfort to the aged."

If the adult student does not find an inspiration to a new and more congenial line of industry, he will find abundant help to increased power and ability in his chosen calling. The increased intelligence he will be able to bring to his task will bring golden returns in increased satisfaction and in increased remuneration.

It will not be amiss to emphasize again the great dual advantages of the study of the Americanized Encyclopedia Britannica through the guidance of the Home Educational Circle—first, the study can be prosecuted at the home, or even at the work-shop, without the aid of expensive teachers or apparatus; second, the self culture which the scholar acquires by studying for himself, digging out for himself the great truths of nature, of science, of production and of commerce, is the best culture of all. What a man learns in that way sticks to him. He does not forget it like lessons learned by rote at school. Let the student not forget that the highest and most profitable learning is the knowledge of ourselves.

THE UNIVERSAL UNIVERSITY

is open, then, and all are welcome. There is no bar of age, sex or condition. Man is never too young nor too old to learn. Dr. Priestley was 40 years old when his attention was directed to the peculiar action of gases escaping from a beer vat, and he began the studies which resulted in his important discoveries in chemistry. Socrates learned to play musical instruments in his old age, and Cato was eighty when he studied the Greek language. Izaak Walton was ninety when he wrote his immortal work, "The Complete Angler," and thousands of other men have done their best work late in life. Genius sometimes blossoms late in life, and no man should let his years discourage him from learning.

But, after all, the world is for the young, and it is to the young that we must address our first instructions.

YOUTHS' DEPARTMENT.

Boys, and girls too, who have life and the world before you, do not let the moments fly idly by. Life seems long, but there is much to accomplish. Youth is the golden age for work and for study as well as for play, and in after years each wasted hour may cause you unavailing regret.

Whatever you know, there is much more to learn; whatever your condition, you may better it. If you are poor and can afford little money and less time for study, you are no worse off than thousands of the wisest and wealthiest men of the day who sprang from poor beginnings. Edison studied telegraphy while a newsboy, and electricity when a telegraph operator. Lincoln and Grant and Garfield were poor boys, and your condition is incomparably better than was theirs, because in the Americanized Encyclopedia Britannica you have an unrivaled text book, a collection of the wisdom of the ages ready at your hand, while they had to trust to scattered and meagre sources of information. They, and others like them though, had industry and determination to succeed, which are qualities far more desired than genius. Bring such qualities with you to the study of the Britannica and you cannot fail to win your way triumphantly in the battle of life. Even if you could fail, your failure would be soothed by the knowledge you would have gained, for learning in itself is one of the highest of earthly goods.   But

YOU WILL NOT FAIL,

for an honest prosecution of the courses of study which will be marked out for you will be a positive insurance against failure.

If you have not made up your mind as to the vocation in life you wish to pursue, a study of some of the subjects mentioned under " General Home Studies " will help to form your choice, or correct a choice un- wisely made.

In connection with those studies, a perusal of the lives of men who have won fame in different walks of life, who have made the world richer by their writings and discoveries, will be found of fascinating interest. They, too, had their troubles to bear, their disappoint- ments to meet, and obstacles to overcome, and the courage with which they overcame, them is one of the most instructive lessons in life.

It may be wise for the young student to enroll him- self first in the biography class, for in the life of some chemist, architect, engineer, lawyer, poet or physician he may find an impulse stimulating him irresistibly to follow the same path in life.

Many of the hundreds of biographies contained in the Britannica are character sermons of the strongest kind which no young man can read without being deeply impressed by their lessons. A good character is as valuable a possession as great learning. To mention some biographies that will splendidly illustrate desir- able elements of character, we recommend—

SOME CHARACTER SERMONS.

For lessons of diligence, application and perseverance, read the lives of Benjamin Franklin, Wellington, Faraday, Garfield, Knight, Cobden, H. Miller, Newton, Scott, Hume, Buffon, Daguerre, Paré, Herschel, Gainsborough and Grant.

To learn of gallant struggles against poverty, sickness and disaster, we advise you to read the lives of Palissy, Hugh Miller, Galileo, Burritt, Carlyle, Bunyan, Tasso, Arkwright, Jacquard, Sir Humphrey Davy, Faraday, Stephenson, Ary Scheffer, Franklin and Andrew Johnson.

For examples of energy, promptitude and hardihood, look into the biographies of Napoleon, Peter the Great, Saladin, Murat, Sheridan, Blaine, Ney, Boulton, Richelieu, Juarez, John Brown, Wellington, H. M. Stanley, Clive, Fr. Xavier, Nelson, Cromwell, A. Jackson and R. E. Lee.

For the manly qualities of patience and fortitude in reverses, peruse the lives of Columbus, Hampden, Dante, Raleigh, Trenck, Kossuth, Sir R. Peel, Tocqueville, Watt, Böttgher, J. Hunter, Audubon, Layard, Addison, Harvey, Henry Wilson, C. Lorraine, Flaxman, West and Pugin.

Pleasant instances of cheerfulness and equanimity of temper may be found in the lives of Goldsmith, Johnson, Sydney Smith, Lord Palmerston and Lincoln.

Lessons of integrity and uprightness of principle are shown in the careers of Diogenes, Newton, Burke, Dr. Arnold, Scott, Sir T. More, W. Chambers, Howard, Handel, Loyola, Horner, Bergh, Emmett, Thierry (A.), Canning, Wilberforce, Stonewall Jackson.

Method, precision, and painstaking — Poussin, Angelo, Cuvier, Titian, Napier, Wordsworth, Brougham, Macaulay, Wellington, Pope, W. Irving, Cecil, Disraeli.

And for the supreme lessons of purity of life and nobility of motive, examine the lives of Wilberforce, Greeley, Lafayette, Garrison, Whittier and other illustrious personages of our own and foreign lands.

Some we have here named might be catalogued, indeed, as types of every excellence that should adorn human character. Such are our own Washington and Benjamin Franklin, but even the youngest student will see how hard it is to attempt a biographical classification on these lines.

THEIR APPLICATION.

By the application of these examples, joined to the influence of home, where they are studied, the earnest, resolute youth can correct the defects of his own character by consciously and unconsciously forming it on the best models. At the same time he will be developing his intellect in every direction. In reading of the life-work of an explorer or navigator he will be learning something of geography, and of commerce; in following the history of a chemist he will be learning something of chemistry from a personal standpoint, always the most interesting manner of approaching any science. It will be strange indeed if some biography does not direct the attention of the learner to some line of study or of action which will become his life-work.

We give, then, some partial lists of men, whose histories appear in the Britannica, who have achieved eminence in some form of endeavor. The classes into which they are divided are by no means all that might be given, and the list is but a small proportion of the names which might be taken from the pages of this incomparable work, but it will do very well for a beginning and the young student can easily prosecute his inquiries farther in any direction.

STUDIES—BIOGRAPHICAL.

ASTRONOMERS.

Arago,
Aristotle,
Bailly,
Copernicus,
Encke,
Galileo,

Halley,
Herschel,
Hind,
Huyghens,
Kepler,
Lagrange,

La Place,
Leverrier,
Newton,
Piazzi,
Tycho Brahe.

BOTANISTS.

Alpini,
Buffon,
Bartram,
Cuvier,
Darwin,

Dodonæus,
Goldsmith,
Gray,
Hooker,
Humboldt,

Huxley,
Linnæus,
Pliny,
Rousseau,
Tyndall.

CHEMISTS.

Bacon, Roger,
Boyle,
Berzelius,
Dalton,
Davy,

Faraday,
Gay-Lussac,
Newton,
Lavoisier,
Liebig,

Paracelsus,
Pasteur,
Playfair,
Priestley,
Silliman.

DRAMATISTS.

Æschylus,
Aristophanes,
Beaumarchais,
Beaumont & Fletcher,
Cibber, Colley,
Congreve,
Corneille,
Dekker,

Dumas, fils,
Foote,
Goldsmith,
Jonson,
Knowles,
Kotzebue,
Molère,
Plautus,

Racine,
Sardou,
Schiller,
Sheridan,
Sophocles,
Van Brugh,
Wycherley.

EXPLORERS AND NAVIGATORS.

Amerigo Vespucci,
Baker,
Balboa,
Belzoni,
Blake,
Bowditch,
Cabots, The,
Cortez,
Columbus,
Cook,
De Long,

De Soto,
Drake,
Du Chaillu,
Franklin,
Fremont,
Frobisher,
Gama, Vasconda,
Hayes,
Hudson,
Kane,

La Salle,
Ledyard,
Livingstone,
Mackenzie,
Nordenskiold,
Parry,
Scoresby,
Speke,
Stanley,
Tasman.

GEOLOGISTS.

Agassiz,	Hayden,	Powell,
Buffon,	Hutton,	Pythagoras
Cuvier,	Lamarck,	Strabo,
Darwin,	Lyell,	Thomson,
Dawson,	Miller,	Tyndall.
Forbes,	Newberry,	

HISTORIANS.

Bancroft,	Herodotus,	Niebuhr,
Bryce,	Hume,	Plutarch,
Buckle,	Irving,	Prescott,
Carlyle,	Knight,	Sismondi,
Froissart,	Layard,	Tocqueville
Froude,	Levy,	Tacitus,
Gibbon,	Macaulay,	Thucydides,
Grote,	Montesquieu,	Voltaire,
Guizot,	Michelet,	Xenophon.
Hazlitt,	Motley,	

INVENTORS AND MECHANICIANS.

Archimedes,	Daguerre,	Palissy,
Arkwright,	Davy,	Rumford,
Bell,	Edison,	Siemens,
Borden,	Ericsson,	Stephenson,
Boyle,	Fulton,	Telford,
Brunel,	Gutenberg,	Watt,
Bunsen,	Morse,	Whitworth.
Colt,		

JURISTS AND LAWYERS.

Bentham,	Curran,	Maine,
Black,	Douglas,	Mansfield,
Blackstone,	Eldon,	Marshall,
Brougham,	Erskine,	Morgan,
Butler,	Fuller,	Stephens,
Calhoun,	Fox,	Story,
Campbell,	Hobbes,	Taney,
Chase,	Jay,	Ulpianus,
Choate,	Kent,	Webster.
Clay,	Lyndhurst,	

MUSICIANS.

Auber,	Gounod,	Scarlatti,
Bach,	Halevy,	Spohr,
Beethoven,	Handel,	Schubert,
Benedict,	Haydn,	Stevenson,
Bennett,	Mendelssohn,	Strauss,
Boildieu,	Meyerbeer,	Sullivan,
Berlioz,	Moore,	Tartini,
Cherubini,	Mozart,	Verdi,
Chopin,	Offenbach,	Vogler,
Cimarosa,	Rossini,	Wagner,
Corelli,	Rubinstein,	Weber.

NOVELISTS.

Balzac,	Gautier,	Reade,
Brontë,	Grimm,	Richter,
Cervantes,	Howells,	Scott,
Cooper,	Hugo,	Smollett,
Daudet,	Irving,	Sterne,
De Foe,	Kingsley,	Stevenson,
Dickens,	Le Sage,	Sue,
Dumas,	Lever,	Swift,
Edgeworth,	Lytton,	Thackeray,
Eliot,	Marryat,	Tolstoi,
Fielding,	Payn,	Trollope.

ORATORS.

Adams, J. Q.,	Cobden,	Grattan,
Antony, Mark,	Conkling,	Hayne,
Beecher,	Danton,	Henry,
Bossuet,	Demosthenes,	Loyson,
Bright,	Depew,	Mirabeau,
Burke,	Disraeli,	O'Connell,
Calhoun,	Douglas,	Pitt,
Chatham,	Everett,	Webster,
Cicero,	Fox,	Whitefield.
Clay,	Gladstone,	

PAINTERS.

M. Angelo,	Cimabue,	Correggio,
Apelles,	Constant,	David,
Botticelli,	Corot,	Delacroix,,

Delaroche,
Dürer,
Gavarni,
Greuze,
Giotto,
Hogarth,
Holbein,
Hunt,
Landseer,

Leonardo da Vinci,
Murillo,
Meissonier,
Raphael,
Rembrandt,
Reynolds,
Rossetti,
Ruysdael,
Rubens,

Stuart,
Teniers,
Titian,
Turner,
Vandyke,
Velasquez,
Watteau,
West.

PATRIOTS.

Adams, Samuel,
Alfred,
Barneveldt,
Bolivar,
Bozzaris,
Garibaldi,

Hampden,
Herminius,
Joan of Arc,
La Fayette,
Kosciusko,
Kossuth,

Lincoln,
Mazzini,
Pym,
Toussaint L'Ouverture,
Wallace,
Winkelried.

PHILOSOPHERS.

Apuleius,
Aristippus,
Aristotle,   .
Aurelius Antoninus,
Bakunin,
Bastiat,
Berkeley,
Cairnes,
Cato,
Comté,
Cousin,
Confucius,

D'Alembert,
Epictetus,
Epicurus,
Fichte,
Fourier,
Hegel,
Hobbes,
Hume,
Lao-tsze,
Lassalle,
Lessing,
Liebnitz,

Plato,
Pythagoras,
Ricardo,
Richter,
Saint Simon,
Schelling,
Schopenhauer,
Seneca,
Smith,
Socrates,
Spinoza,
Whately.

PHYSICIANS AND SURGEONS.

Abercrombie,
Abernethy,
Æsculapius,
Avicenna,
Agnew,
Baillie,
Bell,
Bichat,

Beyer,
Celsus,
Forbes,
Galen,
Gall,
Hahnemann,
Haller,
Harvey,

Hunter,
Huygens,
Jenner,
Owen,
Paracelsus,
Pasteur,
Pliny.

POETS.

Addison,	Cowper,	Milton,
Anacreon,	Dante,	Moore,
Ariosto,	Dryden,	Petrarch,
Bellman,	Firdousi,	Poe,
Beranger,	Gay,	Pope,
Brownings, The,	Goethe,	Schiller,
Bryant,	Goldsmith,	Shakspeare,
Burns,	Hafiz,	Shelley,
Butler,	Heine,	Spenser,
Byron,	Homer,	Tasso,
Camoens,	Hood,	Tennyson,
Campbell,	Horace,	Uhland,
Catullus,	Jonson,	Virgil,
Chatterton,	Keats,	Wieland,
Chaucer,	Longfellow,	Wordsworth.
Coleridge,	Lowell,	

SCIENTISTS.

Agassiz,	Darwin,	Lubbock,
Ampere,	Descartes,	Layard,
Audubon,	Faraday,	Muller,
Brewster,	Guyot,	Napier,
Bunsen,	Huxley,	Pascal,
D'Alembert,	La Grange,	Talbot,
D'Anville,	Legendre,	Tyndall.

SCULPTORS.

Angelo, Michael,	Donatello,	Houdon,
Bartholdi,	Flaxman,	Phidias,
Canova,	Goujon,	Powers,
Cellini,	Hosmer,	Thorwaldsen.

SOLDIERS.

Alexander,	Custer,	Hannibal,
Attila,	Epaminondas,	Jackson, "Stonewall,"
Belisarius,	Eugène,	Kearney, Phil.,
Blucher,	Frederick,	Lee, R. E.,
Cæsar,	Genghiz Khan,	Marlborough,
Charlemagne,	Godfrey de Bouillon,	MacMahon,
Coligni,	Gordon,	Moore, Sir John,
Cromwell,	Grant,	Moreau,
Condé,	Gustavus Adolphus,	Moltke,

Napoleon,
Nelson,
Ney,
Pizarro,
Sulla,

Sheridan,
Sherman,
Themistocles,
Turenne,
Wallenstein,

Washington,
Wellington,
William the Conqueror,
Wolseley,
Xenophon.

STATESMEN.

Adams, John,
Aristides,
Benton,
Bismarck,
Blaine,
Bright,
Brougham,
Burke,
Canning,
Caprivi,
Cavour,
Choiseul,
Clive,
Clarendon,
Cobden,
Dalhousie,

Disraeli,
Derby, E.,
Fillmore,
Franklin,
Gallatin,
Gambetta,
Garfield,
Gladstone,
Hamilton, Alexander,
Henry,
Jackson,
Jefferson,
Macchiavelli,
Madison,
Mazarin,
Metternich,

Mirabeau,
Morris, Robert,
Palmerston,
Parnell,
Peel,
Pitt,
Randolph,
Richelieu,
Salisbury,
Seward,
Sumner,
Talleyrand,
Thiers,
Washington,
Walpole.

THEOLOGIANS AND RELIGIOUS WRITERS.

Á Kempis,
Aquinas,
Athanasius,
Augustine, S.,
Beecher,
Bossuet,
Calvin,
Collier, J.,
Cranmer,
Erasmus,

Everett,
Fuller,
Gibbon,
Huss,
Knox,
Luther,
Melancthon,
Mohammed,
Newman,
Origen,

Pascal,
Parker,
Savonarola,
Swedenborg,
Taylor,
Watts,
Wesley,
Wycliffe,
Zoroaster,
Zwingli.

Readers of the gentler sex need not be told that some of the most noted names in history have been those of women who, as artists, authors or rulers have by force of genius attracted and held the world's attention. The following short list will serve to remind students of a few of the many women who have won renown by their intellect, or reverence and love by softer, diviner qualities:

GIFTED OR FAMOUS WOMEN.

Anne of Austria,	Corday, Charlotte,	Maria Theresa,
Aspasia,	D'Arblay, Mme.,	Mary Stuart, Queen,
Austin, Jane,	Dudevant, Mme.,	Nightingale, Florence,
Bonheur, Rosa,	Eliot, George,	Ossoli, Margaret Fuller,
Bremer, Fredrika,	Elizabeth, Queen,	Pocahontas,
Brontë, Charlotte,	Genlis, Mme. de,	Roland, Mme.,
Browning, E. B. B.,	Grey, Lady Jane,	Sappho,
Catharine de Medici,	Hypatia,	Sevigné, Mme. de,
Catharine, Empress,	Joan of Arc,	Stael, Mme. de,
Cenci, Beatrice,	Marie Antoinette,	Washington, Martha.

> "Lives of great men all remind us
> We can make our lives sublime
> And, departing, leave behind us
> Footsteps in the sands of time."

Longfellow's familiar verse may well recur to the student who peruses the life histories of the renowned persons whose names have been given in the preceding list, or any considerable number of them. Very few of them all had any exceptional advantages to start with. What marked them as men set apart from their fellows, the millions who have gone to their graves leaving no monuments of great achievements behind them, was chiefly their fixedness of purpose and the untiring energy with which they carried it out ; in other words, their willingness and capacity for work. "Genius is infinite capacity for taking pains," according to one definition, and if the student can learn from these biographies the lessons of perseverance and also of patience, they will be well on the high road to success. They, too, can leave behind them footprints in the sands of time. They must not expect success in a moment; it usually comes only after long plodding. Robert Bruce, after years of failure to free Scotland from English rule, hunted for his life, lay in hiding in a cave where he saw a spider trying to clamber up the bare wall. Six times the spider renewed the task, each time falling back to the ground, but the seventh time succeeded. Bruce, who had in despair determined to flee from his country, took the lesson to heart, made one more effort and won.

While reading the lives of these men the student will be insensibly tempted to investigate the subjects they were interested in, and in the list of "General Home Studies," given on a preceding page, he will find a variety to select from, or can turn directly to the pages of the Encyclopedia, where all subjects are arranged in alphabetical order. He can take courses in history, geography, astronomy, geology, chemistry, literature, architecture, agriculture and a host of other sciences and arts, and in so doing doubtless will, almost without intention, select the particular pursuit which he desires to make his life work. Let him remember that all honest work is honorable and that success in any line of work is not to be despised.

RECREATIONS.

But perhaps so much talk of work may tire the young student and there are scores of healthy amusements which, when indulged in to a rational extent, are of actual benefit to the worker by relaxing his mind or strengthening his body. When one's occupation is sedentary, as that of a student, a professional man or many artisans, active exercise is needed daily to keep the body in trim for its work. The Britannica is as complete in this direction as in all others and gives descriptions of many sports which can be indulged in to advantage by the student. Following is a partial list:

GAMES, SPORTS AND PASTIMES.

Angling,	Croquet,	Poker,
Archery,	Draughts,	Quoits,
Athletics,	Euchre,	Rowing,
Backgammon,	Football,	Shooting,
Baseball,	Games,	Skating,
Billiards,	Golf,	Swimming,
Bowls,	Gymnastics,	Tennis,
Bicycling,	Legerdemain,	Whist,
Chess,	Lacrosse,	Wrestling,
Cribbage,	Magic, White,	Yachting.
Cricket,		

By this time every student of the Home Educational Circle will have decided what vocation in life he intends to pursue, and it is desirable to map out courses of study on various special subjects. There is such an endless variety of occupations that it will be necessary to work on general lines to a certain extent. In studying any of the following departments the student should apply the lessons of perseverance and thoroughness he has learned in the biography class, and cheer his work with the reflection that self-culture and success are the privileges of no special rank or class. They are open to all, especially in this glorious republic. Here the plow boy can become the President of the United States; the railroad brakeman, the manager and even the owner of the railroad. The lowest clerk in a little store may become a merchant prince by application and industry, and the greater his knowledge of men and affairs the better will be his prospect of success. Recall the hundreds of examples of men who have reached success, in intellectual achievements, or in amassing wealth, from the most humble beginnings, and resolve to accept no such thing as failure in your chosen calling.

We shall now establish special colleges for the Farmer, the Artisan, the Merchant and the Professional man, representing the four great divisions of activity in civilized life, and the student in any one of these fields will find in the invaluable pages of the Britannica, contributed by the men of most experience in each branch, such a world of information as will give him an unrivalled equipment. The earnest student in the Home Educational Circle can leave the home armed with every weapon to fight the stern battle of life.

AGRICULTURAL DEPARTMENT.

All wealth comes originally from the soil. The farmer bears the weight of the universe upon his shoulders. He is the keystone of civilization. There is justice then in beginning this series of occupations with that of the farmer. And farming, when rightly understood, is both a profession and a science. To be successful the farmer must be something of a naturalist and something of a chemist; he must know what soils are suited to the production of different crops, and he must know what fertilizers are best adapted to aiding in the cultivation of each crop. Farm life is the healthiest and most invigorating in the world when the farmer is intelligent and knows how to produce the best results without exhaustive labor. The time has passed when farming can be successfully conducted without keen intelligence and a thorough scientific knowledge, and the Britannica is rich in information which will enable a man to become a scientific farmer. Brains and ability are fully as necessary in farming as in any other pursuit and the American farmer is not and cannot be the "dull, senseless clod " of the poet. The roll of subjects here given should be diligently studied by the farmer, or the would-be farmer, and he can easily extend the list for himself.

STUDIES—FARMING.

Agrarian Law,	Flour,	Oats,
Agriculture,	Forests,	Oils,
Animals,	Free Trade,	Parasites,
Ant,	Fruit,	Pleuro-pneumonia,
Arboriculture,	Gooseberry,	Potatoes,
Atmosphere,	Grasses,	Poultry,
Banking,	Granges,	Pumpkin,
Barometer,	Guano,	Preserved Food,
Bean,	Heating,	Rent,
Bee,	Honey,	Salts,
Birds,	Hops,	Sequoia,
Botany,	Horse,	Sewage,
Bread,	Hunting,	Sheep,
Breeds,	Hybridism,	Silo,
Building,	Inheritance,	Sugar
Butter,	Insects,	Swan,
Cattle,	Insurance,	Swine,
Cheese,	Irrigation.	Tobacco,
Clover,	Jute,	Transplanting,
Coal,	Labor Laws,	Veterinary Science,
Commerce,	Land,	Vegetable Kingdom,
Cuckoo,	Land Laws,	Vine,
Dairy,	Landlord,	Wages,
Distillation,	Law,	Walnut,
Dog,	Lease,	Warping,
Education,	Maize,	Wheat,
Emigration,	Manure.	Wool,
Ensilage, '	Mensuration,	Zoology.
Flax,	Murrain,	

ARTISAN DEPARTMENT.

If farming is the keystone of civilization, manufacturing is the corner stone. Without the artisan there would be no comforts in life, no luxuries, and not even what we have grown to look upon as necessities. Mankind would still be wearing skins of animals and sleeping in caves. The artisan, the man who works with his hands to fashion or help fashion the endless products of the inventive skill of the ages, occupies a position of importance and dignity. He is a producer in the literal sense of the word.   He can take to his heart the words of Daniel Webster: "Labor is one of the great elements of society, the great substantial interest on which we all stand." A good artisan, a skilled mechanic, has something to be proud of and the more skill he has the greater success he will achieve, the greater advancement.   What the artisan should carefully avoid is the danger of plodding in a single groove, of becoming a mere machine.   Study of the principles on which his work is based and the tools and forces with which he is operating and the materials he is using will enable the mechanic to become more than a mere machine.   Intelligent study and self culture, joined to the practical knowledge which comes from his actual labor, will increase his earning capacity as well as his satisfaction in his work.   Such study will enable him to develop into the foreman, the inventor, the contractor, the employer, the manufacturer.   He may emulate or surpass the Whitneys, the Stephensons, the Franklins, Fultons, McCormicks, Edisons, Bessemers and their like, who were not satisfied with the repetition of a daily task, but were constantly striving to improve old machines or invent new methods.

In aiding the artisan, ambitious of self-culture, there is nothing to approach the Britannica, which will furnish him information on every conceivable subject connected with his trade.   The dyer, cooper, foundryman, printer, miner, carpenter, mason, can all find plentiful stores of knowledge in its magic pages.   For convenience lists of studies have been arranged for workers in wood and workers in metals.

STUDIES—WORKERS IN WOOD, ETC.

Arch,	Beech,	Building,
Architecture,	Bookbinding,	Canoe,
Arithmetic,	Botany,	Carriage,
Atmosphere,	Bridge,	Carving,

Cooperage,
Cork,
Dockyard,
Drawing,
Dyeing,
Enamel,
Encaustic Tiles,
Fire,
Forests,
Fuel,
Furniture,
Glass,
Hammer,

Hand Tools,
Heat,
India Rubber,
Ivory,
Lamp,
Lathe,
Lifts (Elevators),
Lighting,
Machine Tools,
Mahogany,
Measurement,
Mensuration,
Nail,

Oak,
Partition,
Patents,
Pine,
Railways,
Roof,
Saws,
Screw,
Shipbuilding,
Teak,
Tile,
Veneering,
Wood Carving.

STUDIES—WORKERS IN METALS.

Acoustics,
Agate,
Aluminium,
Arch,
Arithmetic,
Arms and Armor,
Arsenal,
Artillery,
Asphalt,
Assaying,
Barometer,
Bell,
Bellows,
Bismuth,
Boiler,
Brass,
Bronze,
Calculating Machines,
Carbon,
Calico Printing,
Case Hardening,
Carving and Gilding,
Clocks,
Coal,
Copper,
Crane,
Cutlery,
Dynamics,

Die Sinking,
Dynamo,
Elasticity,
Electricity,
Electrolysis,
Embossing,
Energy,
Engraving,
Forge,
Furnace,
Geometry,
Gold,
Gold Beating,
Gravitation,
Gunmaking,
Hammer,
Horse Shoeing,
Iron,
Japanning,
Lacquer,
Lathe,
Lead,
Leather,
Locks,
Machine Tools,
Malachite,
Mensuration,
Metallurgy,

Metal Work,
Mineralogy,
Mines,
Nails,
Perpetual Motion,
Plate,
Plated Ware,
Platinum,
Pneumatics,
Pontoons,
Potassium,
Printing Press,
Projection,
Pump,
Safes,
Screws,
Sewing Machines,
Solder,
Steam Engine,
Steel,
Tempering Metals,
Tin,
Tin Plate,
Tricycle,
Valve,
Wire,
Wire Rope.

These subjects need not and, in fact, should not, be studied in alphabetical order, but every artisan can tell for himself what are the elemental subjects of his trade and what are incidental. The artisan will find that a study of the lives of inventors and mechanicians will stimulate his ambition and that his knowledge cannot be too wide or too minute to aid his ambition. Self-culture will be to him a stepping-stone to success.

COMMERCIAL DEPARTMENT.

Without commerce, agriculture and manufacturing would be like a body without arms and legs. Commerce is the connecting link between nations and between men. It is the instinct of barter and sale that has built the roads, railways and ships which make communication possible between all parts of the world. The owner of a little store and the proprietor of a great commercial house employing thousands of men; the expressman and the builder of a railroad, are all, in varying degree, engaged in commerce, and the measure of success attained by each is defined by the skill with which he anticipates or directs the wants of the public and supplies them. The wider his knowledge of materials and of men the more successful is the merchant bound to be, and in this age of keen competition he should lose no opportunity to improve his mental equipment. The man who enters trade must not be content to study price lists but must widen his grasp of affairs by a comprehensive study of all the machinery of business. He cannot gain a personal experience of it all, life would be too short for that, but he can study its principles in books, and nowhere but in the Britannica will he find them all brought together, convenient to his hand.

In any branch of business the man who, by persistent self-culture, has gained a general knowledge, perseverance, resolution, and an accurate realization of his own powers and his own limitations, will be able to far outstrip his competitor who has neglected self-culture. Let the merchant or the young man just starting in a business career, study the Britannica's articles on "Commerce," and follow it up by a study of the other subjects in the following list:

STUDIES—GENERAL COMMERCIAL.

Abandonment,	Corporation,	Railways,
Acceptance,	Credit,	Real Estate,
Account,	Dollar,	Sales,
Adjustment,	Exchange,	Salvage,
Adulteration,	Fairs,	Shipping,
Arithmetic,	Free Trade,	Smuggling,
Assets,	Insurance,	Tariff,
Average,	Interest,	Taxation,
Bankruptcy,	International Law,	Telegraph,
Banks,	Labor,	Telephone,
Bills,	Lotteries,	Textiles,
Bookkeeping,	Mensuration,	Tonnage,
Botany,	Mineralogy,	Trade,
Bullion,	Money,	Trade, Balance of,
Carriers,	Monopoly,	Trade, Boards of,
Coinage,	Numismatics,	'Trades Unions,
Commerce,	Partnership,	Value,
Company,	Patents,	Wages,
Contraband,	Political Economy,	Weights and
Contract,	Post Office,	Measures.
Co-operation,		

BRANCHES OF TRADE.

It will be unnecessary to divide the general subject of commerce into its almost innumerable branches, for they all overlap each other. It is certain, however, that there is no subject of trade that is not clearly treated in the Britannica, and the merchant handling any branch of goods, or the merchant handling hundreds of different articles, as in general and department stores, can find valuable information in this great work on all subjects in which he is specially interested. The dealer can learn new things about the articles he deals in, and in an infinite variety of ways can increase his general information on the subject of trade, and his success in his particular chosen field.

The general subject may be subdivided to fit the needs of dealers into Food Supplies, Personal and Household Effects and Moneys and Values, for bankers, insurance men, etc., and for their use the following tables are recommended.

STUDIES—FOOD, BEVERAGES, ETC.

Alcohol,	Distillation,	Oils,
Ale,	Eggs,	Olives,
Alum,	Fasting,	Orange,
Apple,	Fisheries,	Oysters,
Arrow Root,	Flour,	Potatoes,
Baking, Bread,	Game,	Poultry,
Balsam,	Gastronomy,	Preserved Food,
Beer,	Gelatin,	Rum,
Bees, Honey,	Gooseberry,	Rye,
Breeds,	Grapes,	Salt,
Brewing,	Grasses,	Sugar,
Butter,	Gum,	Tea,
Cheese,	Hops,	Vegetables,
Cherry,	Maize,	Vinegar,
Cocoa,	Malt,	Vines,
Coffee,	Milk,	Water,
Cookery,	Mushroom,	Wheat,
Cotton-seed Oil,	Nutrition,	Wine.
Dietetics,	Oats,	

STUDIES—PERSON AND HOUSEHOLD.

Alpaca,	Arms and Armor,	Book,
Amber,	Asbestos,	Bookbinding,
Aniline,	Bleaching,	Bonnet,

Calico Printing.
Carpets,
Clocks,
Costumes,
Cotton,
Diamonds,
Embroideries,
Engraving,
Feathers,
Fibers,
Fine Arts,
Flax,
Flowers, Artificial,
Fuel,
Fur,
Furniture,
Gems,
Glass,
Glycerine,
Gold,
Gums,

Hat,
Hosiery,
India Rubber,
Ink,
Ivory,
Jewelry,
Kite,
Lace,
Leather,
Linen,
Linoleum,
Manila,
Matches,
Needle,
Oven,
Painting,
Paper,
Paraffin,
Petroleum,
Porcelain,

Pottery,
Ribbons,
Rope,
Seals,
Sewing Machines,
Shoemaking,
Silk,
Soap,
Stove,
Terra Cotta,
Textiles,
Tiles,
Tobacco,
Velvet,
Watches,
Wax,
Weaving,
Wire,
Wool,
Yarn.

STUDIES—MONEY AND VALUES.

Account,
Arithmetic.
Banking,
Bankruptcy,
Bills,
Bookkeeping,
Building,
Bullion,
Calendar,
Check,
Contract,
Commerce,
Co-operation,
Debt,
Decimal Coinage,
Dollar,
Exchange,-
Exchequer,

Excise,
Federal Government,
Finance,
Free Trade,
Gold,
Government,
Guilds,
Insurance:
    Fire,
    Life,
    Marine,
Interest,
Labor Laws,
Law,
Lotteries,
Mining,
Mint,
Money,

Mortgages,
Partnership,
Railways,
Real Estate,
Safe Deposit
        Companies,
Sales,
Savings Banks,
Silver,
Stock Exchange,
Tariff,
Taxation,
Trusts,
Value,
Wages,
Wealth,
Weights and Measures.

PROFESSIONAL DEPARTMENT.

If agriculture is the keystone of civilization the professions are the cap sheaf. In that general term are
comprehended the pursuits of all the arts and of all the
sciences, the intellectual relations of men and of govern-
ments. They have to do with the refinements of life,
and any one of them, approached in the right spirit, is
a fascinating study as well as a means of livelihood.
Here the work of self-culture is never over for there is
always more to learn and with widening knowledge
there will be an ever-increasing zest for learning. Here
perhaps more than in any other field does the Britannica excel all other authorities in the breadth of its
information. It is a rich mine full of virgin gold where
the student can find priceless aid in perfecting himself
for the pursuit of any profession. Lawyer, doctor,
engineer, architect, preacher, chemist or writer, artist
or philosopher, can in these glowing pages find the
cream of all human knowledge, in his special field. The
young man or woman enrolled in the Home Educational
Circle will find through an earnest study of the subjects
here outlined an "open sesame" to success in every
profession. Here more than elsewhere, however, is it
necessary to ponder wisely in making a selection, to
devote your lifetime to a profession for which you have
natural taste and aptitude.

LEGAL.

The law is a noble profession and in the Britannica is
a noble range of subjects for study. From the article
on Law, which should be read first, the student can
proceed to study of the various legal codes and to special articles like those on Marriage, Testamentary,
Commercial, Marine, International and Municipal
Laws. The subjects are presented clearly and concisely

and their study will give the embryo lawyer a better equipment than that of many an eminent advocate or jurist, of whose life he can read in the biographical department, heretofore outlined.

STUDIES—LAW.

Abandonment,	Constitution,	Inheritance,
Abatement,	Constitutional law,	Injunction,
Action,	Contempt of Court,	Insanity,
Admiralty,	Contraband,	Insurance,
Adoption,	Corn Laws,	International Laws,
Adulteration,	Council,	Intestacy,
Advocate,	Court Martial,	Jury,
Affidavit,	Crime,	Labor, Labor Laws,
Agrarian Laws,	Criminal Law,	Land Laws,
Alien,	Damages,	Landlord and Tenant,
Ambassador,	Divorce,	Law,
Annuities,	Emigration,	Libel,
Appeal,	Entail,	Lien,
Apprentice,	Equity,	Limitations,Statute of,
Arbitration,	Evidence,	Liquor Laws,
Arraignment,	Exchange,	Magistrate,
Arrest,	Exchequer,	Medical Jurisprudence,
Assignment,	Excise,	Mortgages,
Assumpsit,	Extradition,	Municipality,
Attachment,	Federal Government,	Murder,
Attorney,	Feudalism,	Navigation Laws,
Balance of Power,	Finance,	Parliament,
Banking,	Fisheries,	Partnership,
Bankruptcy,	Fraud,	Partition,
Bill,	Free Trade,	Patents,
Bookkeeping,	Genealogy,	Penitentiary,
Bribery,	Government,	Police,
Building Societies,	Guilds,	Political Economy,
Calendar,	Habeas Corpus,	Poor Laws,
Canon Law,	Heraldry,	Press Laws,
Casuistry,	History,	Prison,
Code,	Homestead,	Railways,
Commerce,	Husband and Wife,	Real Estate,
Communism,	Infanticide,	Riparian Law,
Company,	Infants,	Roman Law,
Conspiracy,	Information,	Salic Law,

Sea Laws,	Tithes,	Usury,
Search, Right of, .	Tort,	Veto,
Suicide,	Trades Unions,	Wages,
Summary Jurisdiction,	Treason,	War,
Summons,	Treaties,	Will,
Sumptuary Laws,	Trespass,	Witness,
Taxation,	Trust,	Women Laws.

MEDICAL.

Medicine and surgery are staffs on which men lean to an increasing extent. The expert in this dual profession, or in either branch, will always be sure of a bountiful measure of success. There is in the Britannica a copious supply of information on all medical subjects, the principal articles having been written by the profoundest medical scholars, and even the professional man with years of experience will find in them a vast amount of helpful knowledge. To the student of medicine the following Britannica articles will be simply invaluable:

STUDIES—MEDICINE AND SURGERY.

Adulteration,	Beard,	Delirium,
Age,	Biology,	Diabetes,
Alchemy,	Blind,	Dietetics,
Alum,	Botany,	Digestive Organs,
Ambulance,	Bright's Disease,	Diphtheria,
Amputation,	Bronchitis,	Disinfectant,
Anæsthesia,	Capillary Action,	Dislocation,
Anatomy,	Cancer,	Distillation,
Anodyne,	Chemistry,	Drowning,
Antiseptics,	Choral,	Drunkenness,
Apoplexy,	Cholera,	Dysentery,
Asthma,	Circumcision,	Dyspepsia,
Athletics,	Climate,	Ear,
Atmosphere,	Corpulence,	Electricity,
Atrophy,	Cremation,	Elephantiasis,
Arteries,	Croup,	Embryology,
Bacteria,	Cupping,	Epilepsy,
Barometer,	Deaf and Dumb,	Epidermis,
Bath,	Dentistry,	Erysipelas,

Ether,
Eye,
Family,
Fasting,
Fever,
Fire,
Galvanometer,
Gelatin,
Germs,
Giant,
Gladiator,
Glanders,
Glycerin,
Goitre,
Gout,
Gum,
Gymnastics,
Health Resorts,
Heart Disease,
Hernia,
Histology,
Homeopathy,
Hospitals,
Hydrocephalus,
Hydropathy,
Hydrophobia,
Hygiene,
Hysteria,
Influenza,

Insanity,
Jaundice,
Leprosy,
Magnetism, Animal,
Malaria,
Marriage,
Measles,
Meningitis,
Medicine,
Mercury,
Metamorphosis,
Milk,
Narcotics,
Nutrition,
Obstetrics,
Ophthalmology,
Opium,
Paralysis,
Parasitism,
Pathology,
Pharmacy,
Phthisis,
Physiogonomy,
Physiology,
Plague,
Pleurisy,
Pneumonia,
Poisons,
Public Health,

Respiration,
Rheumatism,
Sanitary Science,
Scarlet Fever,
Sewage,
Skeleton,
Skin Diseases,
Sleep,
Small Pox,
Smell,
Spectacles,
Stammering,
Stethoscope,
Stomach
Sunstroke,
Surgery,
Torture,
Touch,
Tourniquet,
Typhoid,
Typhus,
Vaccination,
Vascular System,
Ventilation,
Vesical Disease,
Veterinary Science,
Vivisection,
Water Supply,
Yellow Fever,

Closely allied to the medical profession is the science of chemistry, which is, in fact, in many directions the most practical of sciences. He who has a precise knowledge of the way in which medicines are made will be better able to appreciate their effects on the human system. Chemistry plays an important part, too, in many manufactures and the practical rewards of an expert knowledge of the subject are increasing yearly. The following course will be found both instructive and interesting.

STUDIES—CHEMISTRY.

Aggregation,	Chloral,	Oxides,
Alkali,	Chlorine,	Oxygen,
Ammonia,	Chloroform,	Siphon,
Ammoniac,	Friction,	Spectroscopy,
Analysis,	Gas,	Sulphur,
Aniline,	Heat,	Sulphuric Acid,
Asbestos,	Hydrogen,	Tannin,
Atom,	Mercury,	Tartaric Acid,
Bunsen Burner,	Molecule,	Turpentine,
Blow Pipe,	Nitrogen,	Ultramarine,
Carbolic Acid,	Nitro Glycerine,	Vacuum,
Carbon,	Oxalic Acid,	Variation and Selection
Chemistry,		

ENGINEERING.

The power to wield and direct the mighty forces of nature, to turn rivers from their courses, to annihilate space and time, to work wonders with steam and electricity is a fascinating possession. The young man who desires to follow any of the numerous branches of engineering has an interesting future before him. Like Archimedes he can say that if he had a lever long enough he could move the earth, and perhaps he can get the lever. At least there are more ways than one of moving the world.

The term engineering is a broad one. There are mining engineers, railroad engineers, military engineers and electrical engineers. There are others, but no matter how many there are, it is certain that they can all find profit and instruction in the pages of Britannica. There are certain general subjects that should be mastered by the followers of all branches of engineering, and they, with many special topics, will be found in the appended list, which is by no means exhaustive. When they have been mastered, the student will be easily able to follow the science of engineering much farther without leaving the Home Educational Circle, by looking up other subjects referred to in the articles mentioned.

STUDIES—ENGINEERING AND MECHANICS.

Acoustics,
Aëronautics,
Air Engines,
Air pumps,
Algebra,
Anchor,
Annealing Glass,
Aqueduct,
Arch,
Archæology,
Architecture,
Artesian Wells,
Asphalt,
Atmosphere,
Atoms,
Attraction,
Balance,
Ballast,
Barometer,
Barracks,
Baths,
Block Machinery,
Bore,
Brake,
Brick,
Bridges,
Bronze,
Building,
Calender,
Cantilever,
Calculating Machines,
Canal,
Climate,
Coal,
Compass,
Conic Sections,
Crane,
Diving,
Dock,
Drawing,
Dynamics,
Dynamite,

Electricity,
Embankment,
Euclid,
Explosives,
Fire,
Flight,
Flying Machines,
Forests,
Fortifications,
Fuel,
Furnace,
Galvanometer,
Gas,
Geodesy,
Geology,
Geometry,
Glass,
Granite,
Gravitation,
Gun Cotton,
Gun Powder,
Gutta Percha,
Gyroscope,
Hammer,
Harbors,
Heating,
Hydro-mechanics,
Ice,
India Rubber,
Iron,
Labor,
Lifts,
Lighthouse,
Magnetism,
Marble,
Mathematical Drawing
    and Modeling,
Mathematics,
Measurement,
Mensuration,
Mercury,
Metallurgy, .

Metal Work,
Mineralogy,
Mining,
Nitroglycerin,
Observatory,
Patents,
Petroleum,
Phosphorus,
Pneumatic,
Pontoons,
Projections,
Pump,
Pyramid,
Pyrometer,
Radiation,
Railways,
River,
River Engineering,
Roads and Streets,
Rope,
Screw,
Seismometer,
Sewerage,
Signals,
Smoke,
Smoke Abatement,
Sponges,
Statistics,
Strength of Materials,
Sulphur,
Surface,
Surveying,
Teak,
Technical Education.
Telemeter,
Telescope,
Thermodynamics,
Thermometer,
Tides,
Torpedo,
Traction, Electric,
Tramway,

Transit Circle,	Turnpike Roads,	Windlass,
Triangulation,	Ventilation,	Wind Mills,
Trigonometry,	Vault,	Wire Rope,
Tunneling,	Water Supply,	Zinc.

If the student's thirst for scientific knowledge is not satisfied by researches in engineering, chemistry, etc., the Britannica will be no less valuable in furnishing him with information on astronomy, biology, botany, meteorology, zoölogy and other sciences, with subordinate topics, to which the following list will be found a serviceable guide:

STUDIES—OTHER SCIENCES.

Abiogenesis,	Geometry,	Protozoa,
Aberration,	Glacial Period,	Psychology,
Adaptation,	Graphotype,	Submarine Telegraphy,
Adhesion,	Gunpowder,	Telegraph,
Anatomy,	Heating,	Telephone,
Aurora Borealis,	Metallurgy,	Telescope,
Astronomy,	Meteorology,	Thermometer,
Bacteria,	Microscope,	Thunder Storm,
Biology,	Mnemonics,	Tides,
Climatology,	Moon,	Tornado,
Compass,	Navigation,	Torpedo,
Conductor,	Nebular Theory,	Traction, Electric,
Conic Sections,	Observatory,	Triangulation,
Comet,	Ornithology,	Transit Circle,
Corona,	Parallax,	Trigonometry,
Darwinian Theory,	Parallels,	Variable Complex,
Dynamics,	Phonograph,	Vascular System,
Eclipse,	Phosphorescence,	Wave,
Earthquake,	Phonetics,	Wave Theory of Light.
Electricity,	Phrenology,	Weber's Law,
Electric Light,	Physiology,	Zodiac,
Geodesy,	Pisciculture,	Zoology.
Geology,	Pneumatics,	

ARTISTIC.

The heaven-born instinct to paint pictures or model statues in clay cannot be taught, but, having that instinct, it must be cultivated assiduously by learning the principles of the arts of painting and sculpture and by studying from the best models. Here self-culture is supreme, for it develops individuality, which should be the aim of every artist. The world has little praise for the artist who is a mere copyist, however great his gifts. But given the artistic gift, lack of means or of time need not dishearten the struggling student. Some of the greatest artists of the world have had to struggle against as great or greater odds, and they did not have the inestimable benefits which the Britannica and the Home Educational Circle offer to the student of today by bringing within his reach the principles of the arts, a vast amount of information on subordinate topics, and the instructive examples given by the lives of great painters, sculptors, architects and musicians. These arts are enchanting subjects of study because they typify all that is most beautiful in nature. They can be studied at the home with the greatest convenience. There is no caste in art. The humblest can become the greatest. Some of the most famous artists have risen from low beginnings, and genius is the only test. The following subjects should be carefully read by the student:

STUDIES—THE ARTS AND MUSIC.

ARTS.

Academy,	Art,	Chemistry,
Æsthetics,	Basilica,	Chiar-oscuro,
Alhambra,	Birds,	Church,
Altar,	Botany,	Column,
Amphitheater,	Bronze Age,	Cornice,
Anatomy,	Building,	Costume,
Angel,	Butterflies,	Crayon,
Arabesque,	Cartoon,	Cross,
Arch,	Carving,	Curve,
Archæology,	Castle,	Demonology,
Architecture,	Catacombs,	Drawing,
Armor,	Cathedrals,	Effigies,

Encaustic Tiles,	Jewelry,	Renaissance,
Painting,	Lithography,	Rome,
Engraving,	Magic,	Romanticism,
Fine Arts,	Mirrors,	Round Towers.
Flags,	Mosaics,	Royal Society,
Florence,	Mural Decoration,	Schools of Painting,
Frescoes,	Numismatics,	Sculpture,
Gems,	Painting,	Stereoscope,
Heraldry,	Photography,	Technical Schools,
History,	Phrenology,	Temple,
Indigo,	Physical Science.	Theater,
Ink,	Physiology,	Venice,
Inscriptions,	Pigments,	Zoölogy,
Ivory,	Poetry,	

MUSIC.

Accent,	Choir,	Music Box,
Acoustics,	Conservatory,	Organ,
Automaton,	Dance,	Piano,
Bagpipe,	Glee,	Speech Sounds,
Ballads,	Guitar,	Trombone,
Bell,	Harmonic Analysis,	Trumpet,
Cantata,	Harp,	Tuning Fork.
Chant,	Lyre,	Violin,
Chime,	Music,	Voice.

LITERARY.

Literature is a wide realm of thought and learning. Taken as a profession, in however restricted a sense, it would still be too wide a field for any man, however bright a genius, to hope to excel in all, or very many of its branches. Poetry, the drama, romance, history, essays, philosophy—it is a life work usually to achieve honor and distinction in any one of them. When we include teaching, journalism, preaching, as well we may do, the field becomes as wide as the universe, as all human learning. The follower of this profession can sup at every flower of human knowledge. "Of making many books there is no end," and the student should let his self-culture be deep and broad and be sure of his ability to add something to the stock of knowledge or put some the world already has in a new and more attractive form, before he succumbs to the temptation to join the ranks of writers. When he can do that he will not lack a welcome from the reading world.

To a certain extent these studies include all others that have been mentioned in the preceding courses. The litterateur, the newspaper man and the teacher are usually expected to know everything or a little of everything. The subjects laid down in the following courses might be mastered to begin with.

STUDIES—LITERATURE AND TEACHING.

Academy,	Charade,	Greek Literature,
Æsthetics,	Church History,	Heraldry,
Alphabet,	Cid,	History,
American Literature,	Conjugation,	Hymns,
Analogy,	Copyright,	Institute of France,
Anthology,	Creeds,	Journalism,
Apocalyptic Literature,	Cryptography,	Kindergarten,
Acrostic,	Dictionary,	Knighthood
Alexandrian School,	Dogmatics,	and Chivalry,
Allegory,	Drama,	Latin Language,
Alliteration,	Dreams,	Libraries,
Americanisms,	Druidism,	Metaphysics,
Art,	Education,	Mysticism,
Astrology,	Encyclopedia,	Newspapers,
Athens,	England, Lang. & Lit.,	Numerals,
Augurs,	Epigram,	Paleography,
Augustan Age,	Epitaph,	Pantomime,
Ballads,	Ethics,	Periodicals,
Bible,	Examinations,	Philosophy,
Bibliography,	Fine Arts,	Poetry,
Book,	Folk Lore,	Press Laws,
Brahmanism,	France, Lang. & Lit.,	Provencal
Buddhism,	Gaelic Lang. & Lit.,	Lang. & Lit.,
Caricature,	Games,	Reporting,
Category,	Germany, Lang. & Lit.,	Rhetoric,
Celtic Literature,	Grammar,	Romance,

Roman Law,
Roman Literature,
Salutations,
Sanskrit,
Satire.
Scandinavian
    Lang. & Lit.

Scholasticism,
Scotch Literature,
Semitic Lang. & Lit.,
Sonnet,
Sophists,   •
Speech Sounds,
Syriac Literature,

Tales,
Talmud,
Technical Education,
Typography,
Universities,
Witchcraft,
Zend Avesta,

STUDIES--PHILOSOPHY.

Agnosticism,
Analysis,
Analytic Judgment,
Aristotle.
Apologetics,
A Priori and A
    Posteriori,

Gnosticism,
Kant,
Metempsychosis,
Monachism,
Neoplatonism,
Peripatetics,
Philosophy,

Plato,
Rationalism,
Skepticism,
Socialism,
Sophists,
Spiritualism.

STUDIES--THEOLOGY AND RELIGION.

Anabaptist,
Anthropomorphism,
Apostolic Fathers,
Apotheosis.
American Church.
Baptists,
Belief,
Bible,
Candlemas,
Canticles,
Cardinal,
Carthusians,
Catechism,
Catechumens,
Catholic Apostolic
    Church,
Confession,
Confirmation,
Congregationalism,
Conclave,
Council,

Creeds,
Diocese,
Dogmatic,
Dunkers,
Eschatology,
Excommunication,
Gospels,
Heresy,
Immaculate
    Conception,
Image Worship,
Independent Religion,
Incense,
Inspiration,
Lutheran Church,
Methodism,
Missal,
Mission,
Mormous,
Mysticism,
Oneida Community,

Popedom,
Presbyterianism.
Purgatory,
Quakers,
Reformation,
Roman Catholic
    Church,
Sacrifice,
Talmud,
Temporal Power,
Theology,
Theosophy,
Theism,
Totemism,
Trappists,
Trent, Council of,
Unitarianism,
United Presbyterian
    Church,
Universalist Church,
Vatican Council.

If the student who has read these pages will now turn them rapidly over, glancing at the numerous tables of articles on the various subjects: biography, commerce, the professions, the arts, the sciences, etc., he will have an increased idea of the possibilities open to the student of the Americanized Encyclopedia Britannica in the Home Educational Circle. He will realize that it was no idle boast to say that the Britannica comprehends all knowledge and lays it before the student in the most convenient form. He will begin to see its great possibilities as an aid to self-culture and to success in any line of work. Equipped with such a store of learning, or only with what applies particularly to his own particular field, the student can go out into the world confident of his ability to succeed.

The battle for proficiency must be his own fight. A great point to be aimed at is to get the working quality well trained. When that is done, the race will be found comparatively easy, and what difficulties and obstacles can be surmounted!

No brave soul is deterred by obstacles. Where there is difficulty, the individual man must come out for better or for worse. Encounter with it will train his strength, and discipline his skill. The road to success may be steep to climb, and it puts to the proof the energies of him who would reach the summit. By experience a man soon learns that obstacles are to be overcome by grappling with them; that the nettle feels as soft as silk when it is boldly grasped; and that the most effective help towards realizing an object is the moral conviction that we can and will accomplish it.

If there were no difficulties there would be no success: if there were nothing to struggle for, there would be nothing to be achieved.

Formed on the best examples, ripened on the best learning, the student of the Home Educational Circle will have a magnificent outfit for his life-work. Facility will come with labor, and the principles he has learned will become more thoroughly his own when he is putting them in practice. Let him not forget, either, that the Home Educational Circle never graduates its students. Its curriculum is as long as life itself, for there is always more to learn and the home will always remain the ideal place for learning.

ALL THINGS POSSIBLE.

If there are still those who doubt the possibility of mastering the arts and sciences without the aid of expensive apparatus and the oral guidance of learned professors in schools and colleges; if there are still those who fear their ability to acquire knowledge and culture through their own efforts, who, in a word, consider "self-culture" a meaningless phrase, we address to them a few earnest words in parting, for they are sadly in need of help to recover from their monstrous error.

There is no doubt that schools and colleges and learned professors make education much easier. If they have a fault it is in making the acquirement of knowledge too easy. Students who know that all difficult points will be explained to them, acquire the habit of leaning too much on their instructors, because it is so much easier than digging things out for themselves. For that reason facts we learn for ourselves remain with us, become part of our equipment, while the same things, learned in school, are very frequently forgotten. Such learning is superficial. So it will be seen that self-culture has a great advantage over the culture of schools and colleges, not in spite of its greater difficulties, but because of them. We prize most that which costs us most pains and trouble to obtain.

Teachers are necessary in childhood to impart elementary studies, but the idea that at a later period their help is requisite for the learning of a science, art, or language, is a mischievous delusion. From the hour when a boy can read his mother-tongue he has it absolutely in his power, without classes, teachers or school buildings, to master all the learning of the world. By this is not meant that life would be long enough for such a purpose, literally, but as long as life lasts a person with ordinary mental capacity and industry can master all things he has time to undertake.

In all ages this great possibility has cheered the poor and the friendless and enabled them, with industrious study, to take their places in history among the learned men of the world. It is more than ever possible now when such a great work as the Americanized Encyclopedia Britannica collects for the student, from all sources, and all parts of the world, all sciences and arts, the information which he would never have either time or means to seek out from its scattered original sources. By its aid thousands of young men are being enabled to prepare themselves by home study for mechanical, mercantile and professional pursuits even more thoroughly than they could do by attending school or colleges. The formation, by the publishers of this great work, of the Home Educational Circle, is in response to the universal silent prayer of young men so situated, for some means of educating themselves. Such an opportunity has never before been offered, and the eagerness with which it is being seized shows both the great need and the great appreciation.

Self-culture is not a meaningless phrase, but a living, . breathing reality. It enlarges the ideals, elevates the thoughts and ennobles the labor of its possessor, no matter how commonplace or humble that labor may be. It gives a zest to life, a joy to the daily round of labors, which nothing can give so well as the constant intercourse with the great minds of the past and the great thoughts and intellectual movements of the present. Be he poor in all else, the possessor of self-culture can count himself rich in the best of all riches.

If, in spite of all his training, the student cannot reap that measure of success which he would like, the habits of study which he will have formed will be the best and dearest solace for any material disappointments. Learning is a prize for its own sake alone as well as for the rewards it will bring and, perhaps, the happiest of all men are those who, putting the ambitions of the world behind them, devote their lives to the delights of study.

Self-culture is, after all, its own best reward. Other rewards will surely come, but the faithful student of the Home Educational Circle need have no regrets that he has not made the most of life.